H46 050 514 5
D1362891
Hertfordshire
HERTFORDSHIRE LIBRARY SERVICE
WITHDRAWN FOR SALE

UNIVERSITY PRESS

CAMBRIDGE UNIVERSITY PRESS
Cambridge, New York, Melbourne, Madrid, Cape Town, Singapore, São Paulo, Delhi

Cambridge University Press
The Edinburgh Building, Cambridge CB2 8RU, UK

www.cambridge.org
Information on this title: www.cambridge.org/9780521732246

First published 2009

Printed in India by Thomson Press (India) Limited

Typeset by Aptara Inc.
Map artwork by Malcolm Barnes

A catalogue record of this book is available from the British Library

ISBN 978-0-521-73224 6 paperback
ISBN 978-0-521-73225 3 paperback plus 2 audio CDs

Contents

Characters

Annie, Leo, Nigel, Simon, Pete: people in the Big Eye competition
Big Eye: different voices who give instructions to the people in the Big Eye House
Violet Carlton: a TV presenter

About the story

Big Eye is a fictional reality TV programme about young people living together for forty days in the Big Eye House.

The young people have been chosen – out of thousands – to be on the programme and stay in the Big Eye House. They cannot see or talk to anyone outside the House and there are cameras that watch almost everything they do. People at home can watch it all on their televisions. They can also phone up to say who they want to leave the House. On Leaving Night, one person has to leave the Big Eye House and is out of the competition. The last person in the House after forty days wins a lot of money – £70,000.

The Big Eye House

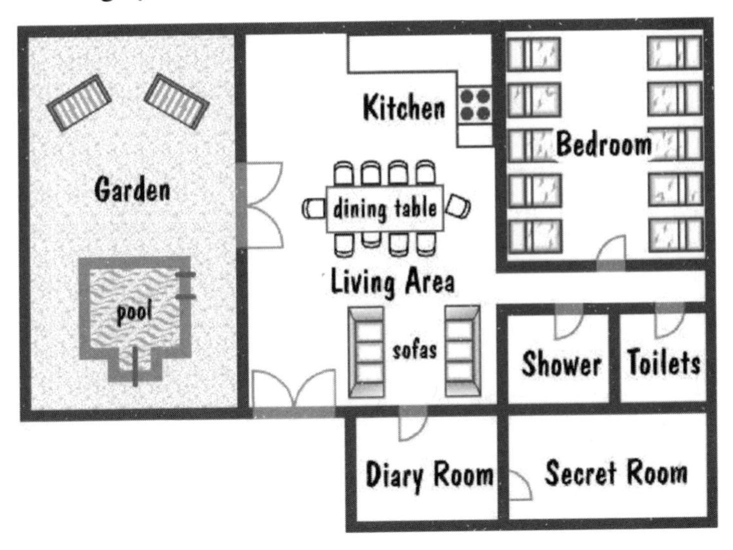

Chapter 1 *The carrot flower*

It's not every day that you wake up to find a carrot on your bed. But that's what happened to me on Day Thirty-Six of my stay in the House.

Well, it wasn't a carrot exactly; it was a flower. A flower cut carefully out of a carrot with a knife. I know it sounds a bit odd, but it was really beautiful, honestly. I felt pleased that somebody had taken the trouble to make it for me. But I had no idea who that 'somebody' might be. I knew who I *wanted* it to be though – Simon. Simon had beautiful hands, along with a beautiful body and a handsome face. But were they hands that could make such a flower? I hoped so.

Looking around the bedroom, I saw that Leo was still in bed. There was one bedroom for all of us in the House with ten beds in it. But no-one was using five of the beds any more, since five people had already left the House. I looked at Leo sleeping. Big Eye turns the lights on in the bedroom at eight o'clock every morning, but that doesn't wake Leo up. Nothing wakes Leo up until he wants to wake up. So he can't have made the flower, I thought. It wasn't the kind of thing he'd do anyway. Leo prefers talking to doing.

Suddenly a voice filled the room. 'This is Big Eye. Would Annie come to the Diary Room please?'

The Diary Room was the place we went to for private conversations with Big Eye. Well, they were private because the other people in the House couldn't hear what you said. But actually they were very public, because everyone watching the *Big Eye* programme on TV could see and hear you. But you usually forgot about that.

Putting on my dressing gown, I put the carrot flower carefully in my pocket. For some reason I wanted to keep it a secret, although I knew this was silly. Thousands, or maybe even millions, of television viewers had already seen me find it.

'Morning, guys.' Out in the main living area, Pete and Nigel were making breakfast. They smiled at me.

'Morning, Annie.'

I looked at both of them as I walked towards the Diary Room. Nigel was a very intelligent man, but he wasn't very good with his hands. I couldn't imagine him being able to make my carrot flower. Pete was an engineer though. Maybe it was him?

I looked out of the window, searching for Simon. There he was, jogging as usual. Every morning, he ran for an hour before breakfast. He'd already worn out some of the grass in the small garden. By the time the competition ended on Saturday there probably wouldn't be any grass left at all. Had Simon taken some time off from his exercise to make my presents? It would be very nice if he had – very nice indeed.

Smiling to myself, I pressed the button on the wall outside the Diary Room door. As I waited for the door to open, I continued watching Simon. If the women watching the programme were anything like me, then Simon and his beautiful body had an excellent chance of winning this competition. The winner would be the person who managed to stay in the House the longest. And the prize for the winner was £70,000. Now there were only four days left until the competition was over.

On Leaving Night thousands of people phoned the TV station to vote – to say which person they wanted to leave the House. At first, Leaving Nights had taken place once a week, on Saturdays. And five people had left the Big Eye House. But now the competition was almost over, there were going to be two extra Leaving Nights. By Saturday, the last day of the competition, there would only be three people left.

Leaving Nights were always the same. Everyone in the House had to sit on the sofas and wait for Violet Carlton, the TV presenter, to tell us who was leaving. So far Simon had always been safe – he hadn't got many votes at all. Neither had I actually. Very few people had phoned to say either of us should leave. I don't know why I was popular. I'm not ugly, but I'm certainly not beautiful.

I was still staring at Simon when I heard the door to the Diary Room start to open. I began to walk into the room. I didn't realise that the door wasn't open wide enough for me to be able to go in. My arm hit the door.

'Ow!' I said, holding my hurt arm. Pete and Nigel looked over.

'OK, Annie?' Pete asked.

'Yes,' I said. 'Just another injury.' All the men were used to me having accidents. I was always dropping something or falling over something.

I was still holding my arm as I sat down on the chair in the Diary Room. Or rather, *in* the chair, because it's so big and so soft you have to half-lie on it. It's impossible to sit in it without relaxing. I think Big Eye knows we'll be more open about what we say if we're relaxed.

'Good morning, Annie,' said Big Eye.

I was halfway through a yawn. 'Good morning, Big Eye,' I said, smiling at the camera in front of me. Big Eye had four or five different voices, depending on what time it was. Sometimes Big Eye was a *he*, and sometimes Big Eye was a *she*. This morning it was the man with the soft voice, a voice like milk chocolate. I liked him.

'And how are you feeling this morning, Annie?' Big Eye asked.

'Fine,' I said, still smiling. 'Very good, in fact.'

'Is there any special reason why you're feeling so good this morning, Annie?'

I could feel the carrot flower under my fingers in my pocket. I knew Big Eye wanted me to talk about it, but I still wanted to keep it to myself. 'Well, things are quite peaceful in here at the moment, I suppose,' I said.

'And why do you think that is, Annie?' asked Big Eye.

I thought about it. 'I suppose it's because Janine and Gloria have gone,' I said. 'They made a lot of trouble, those two.'

Janine and Gloria had both been very loud people. *Obvious* people. As well as the prize money for the winner, there was £10,000 for anyone who had a romance in the House. Both Janine and Gloria had tried very hard to have a romance with Simon.

'Is there any other reason why you feel so good this morning, Annie?' asked Big Eye.

I looked at the camera. It seemed as if Big Eye wasn't going to give up. 'Yes,' I said at last. 'You know there is. Somebody left me a present again. Yesterday it was that beautiful paper boat, and today it was … this.' I brought the carrot flower out of my pocket and held it in my hand in front of the camera. 'It's lovely, isn't it?'

Big Eye didn't give an opinion. Big Eye *never* gave opinions. 'Do you know who gave you this present, Annie?'

I shook my head. 'No, I don't. It's a complete mystery. I tried to find out who made me the paper boat yesterday, and nobody would admit to it. So I don't know who my secret present-giver is.' Then I realised something, and looked at the camera, wide-eyed. 'But *you* know, don't you? You must do. You know what's going on all over the House.'

The Big Eye House has cameras everywhere, except for inside the shower and the toilets. The cameras can even see us at night – there are special cameras that work in the dark.

'Who is it?' I asked Big Eye. 'Who's been leaving me these presents?'

'Big Eye cannot give you that information, Annie,' Big Eye said.

'You mean you don't *want* to,' I said.

Big Eye stayed silent. I put the carrot flower back into my pocket, suddenly realising (I'm a bit slow in the mornings before I've had a cup of strong coffee) that if Big Eye knew who was giving me the presents, then everybody knew. That was, everybody in the United Kingdom who was watching the *Big Eye* programme. It was very strange to think that millions of people knew more about what was happening to me than I did myself.

'How does it feel to be the only woman left in the House, Annie?' Big Eye asked.

I thought about it. 'Well, I suppose I'm not sure what the men really think of me any more. I mean, they're being very nice to me, but how do I know if they really like me or not? Maybe they're just being nice to me because they want to start a romance and win £10,000.'

'And how do you feel about having a romance with someone in the House?' Big Eye asked next.

I immediately thought about Simon and smiled to myself. 'I'm not sure,' I said to Big Eye. 'The men left are all very different, aren't they? I like some things about all of them.'

There was a pause. Big Eye often leaves pauses. He wants you to feel uncomfortable so you say anything just to fill the silence. I don't mind silence myself. I think that comes from working in a museum. Museums can be quite silent places, especially in the summer. People don't want to look at old pictures and furniture when the sun is out.

'Big Eye has some instructions for you now, Annie,' Big Eye said.

'Oh?' I said and waited.

'You are to tell Leo, Simon, Pete and Nigel that Big Eye wishes them to write a poem for you. This poem should say how they feel about you.'

'A poem?' I said, feeling suddenly annoyed that I only had a camera to look at. I wanted to be able to stare Mr Milk Chocolate right in the face. 'You mean like:

Roses are red,
Violets are blue,
Sugar is sweet
And so are you?'

'Everyone is allowed to decide what type of poem they want to write themselves,' Big Eye said.

'They'll hate it!' I said, not looking forward to going out there and telling them all.

Big Eye continued, obviously not worried about how the men might feel. 'They must complete their poems by ten-thirty this morning,' he said. 'At eleven o'clock you will read the poems out and decide which poem is the best. The poems should be anonymous – nobody should sign their poem and you should not know who has written them. This is the task for today.'

Every day we were given something to do – a task. This was partly to keep us busy, but mostly to interest the viewers at home. Some people enjoyed just watching us cleaning the House or chatting to each other by the pool in the garden. I have no idea why. But most people wanted to see us doing silly things. While I'd been in the House I'd dressed up as a horse with Simon, taken part in a singing competition (I came last), and had a girls against boys water fight in the garden (the boys won). We had to do what Big Eye told us – those were the rules of the Big Eye competition.

'Big Eye would like you to go and tell the others about today's task now, Annie,' Big Eye told me. I pushed myself out of the chair.

'OK then,' I said. 'Bye for now.'

'Goodbye, Annie,' Big Eye said.

I left the Diary Room to go and break the bad news to the guys.

Chapter 2 *As blue as the sea*

It's difficult to describe what it was like, living in the House. You didn't exactly forget your life outside – your friends, your family, your job – but they almost felt like a story you'd heard. The House was the reality – with its rooms, people, and Big Eye telling us what to do.

You even forgot about the cameras most of the time. I know that probably sounds unbelievable, but you did. There were so many of them everywhere, recording every little thing we did or said. But you got so used to it; you stopped thinking about it. We were like fish swimming around in a bowl, except it was a bowl we couldn't see out of. We didn't know what was happening in the world outside. The House, and what happened in it, was our world. Which is why something like a stupid competition to write a poem became so important.

When I broke the news about the task, none of the guys seemed very happy about it, but Nigel was especially annoyed. 'That's not fair!' he complained, after I'd described what Big Eye wanted them to do. 'I don't even like writing shopping lists! I wouldn't even know how to *begin* to write a poem. And *he's* a writer already.' Nigel pointed at Leo, who had climbed out of bed five minutes before, when Big Eye had ordered everybody to meet on the sofas. He was holding onto the mug of coffee Pete had made him as if it were life-saving medicine.

'I write detective stories, not poems,' he said with a yawn. 'And anyway, I have to be really interested in something to want to write.'

'You mean you have to be inspired?' Pete asked.

Leo nodded, drinking some of his coffee. 'That's right. I have to be inspired.'

'And you feel more inspired by a dead body than by Annie?' asked Simon, looking over at me. 'That's not very nice, is it, Annie?'

Leo smiled at me. 'Sorry, Annie, I'm afraid it's true. Blood, fear and mystery – that's what I'm inspired by.'

I felt annoyed, but tried not to show it. Out of all the men in the House, Leo was the one who had made the least effort to get me to like him. He was the same with everybody though – Leo was just Leo, and we could take him or leave him. But somehow we liked him anyway. He was very sociable, and even though he could be lazy, he was also funny and interesting. I didn't think Leo had ever had to try very hard with people.

'Well,' I said, 'I hope you're all going to co-operate. You've all got to do the task, so there's no point in complaining. You know what will happen if you don't.'

'No nice food,' Nigel said.

Big Eye gave us the very basic food we needed, like bread, rice and potatoes, but we had to earn anything more than that by doing these tasks successfully.

'And it's Tuesday today,' Nigel went on.

'Takeaway night!' said Pete.

On Tuesdays, if we'd achieved our task, Big Eye gave us beer and a takeaway meal from an Indian or a Chinese restaurant. We all enjoyed takeaway night. Even Simon, who usually only ate healthy food.

'We'd better get busy then!' said Leo, and he went back towards the bedroom, taking his cup of coffee with him.

'Don't forget – no names on the poems. They must be anonymous,' I called after him.

The others went out into the garden. When I tried to follow them, Simon told me to stay indoors. 'I won't be able to think properly if you're around,' he said. 'I'll feel too stupid.'

'Me too,' agreed Pete. 'Sorry, Annie.'

'That's OK,' I said. 'I'll do a bit of cleaning. This place is a mess.'

It was true. Janine had been the one who liked cleaning. When she hadn't been trying to get Simon alone, she had been busy with the hoover or washing the kitchen floor. It had been a bit annoying at the time – you couldn't put your coffee cup down for a moment without Janine taking it away to wash it up. But now she wasn't with us any more and the place was getting dirty, I missed her. Well, to be honest, I missed the work she had done, not her. She hadn't been very nice to me at all.

As I got the hoover out and got started, I was still thinking about how the guys had taken the news about the task. None of them had wanted to do it. While I knew it wasn't easy to write poems, I did feel they might at least have pretended that I was a good subject for a poem. But as it was, they had all complained about it. Leo had even said he would rather write about dead bodies. None of which was very good for a girl's confidence.

I was so busy feeling sorry for myself as I worked that I didn't notice what was happening. The hoover had 'eaten' the edge of the carpet and was beginning to make a very strange noise.

'Oh no!' I said worriedly, trying to pull the hoover away, but it wouldn't come free. The edge of the carpet was stuck inside the hoover. The noise was deafening – the hoover sounded as if it was going to explode. I bent over to try to pull the carpet free, but I couldn't. Then suddenly the hoover stopped screaming.

I looked round. Leo had turned the hoover off at the plug in the wall and was standing laughing at me. 'I know I said I was inspired by murder, Annie,' he said, 'but what has that carpet ever done to you?'

I looked at him, speaking crossly because I was embarrassed. 'Shouldn't you be writing your poem?' I asked.

Leo walked over to the kettle and turned it on. 'Finished it,' he said.

I stood up, leaving the hoover where it was. I'd had quite enough of cleaning for one morning. 'That was a bit quick,' I said.

Leo just smiled. 'Do you want a coffee?' he asked.

Suddenly a coffee was the thing I wanted more than anything else in the world. What had I been thinking of, trying to do the cleaning without a cup of coffee inside me first? No wonder it had all gone wrong. 'Oh yes, please!' I said.

But Leo had left the kettle and gone over to the sofa to sit down. 'Two sugars in mine,' he said. 'And not too much milk.'

'Leo!' I said. 'I thought you were offering to make *me* a cup of coffee!'

He laughed. 'I know,' he said.

That was just like Leo. I don't know how he did it. If any of the other guys had tried such a joke on me I'd have felt really cross. But somehow I found myself laughing with Leo and going off to make the coffee. If anybody got away with murder, it was Leo.

'There you are,' I said, coming back with the coffee. 'You're lucky I'm not throwing it at you.'

Leo smiled and took his coffee. 'I *am,* aren't I?' he said. 'With all the accidents you have. How do you manage to do your job?'

'What do you mean?' I asked.

'Well,' he said, 'museums are full of valuable stuff, right? And you have accidents all the time. Don't you keep on breaking things?'

I *had* broken a very old plate once, but I wasn't going to tell Leo and everyone watching the programme about that. My boss still hadn't forgotten about it, and neither had I. 'I don't get to touch the things in the museum very often,' I told Leo. 'My job is to introduce the museum to groups of schoolchildren who visit for the day.'

Leo laughed. 'You mean you say, "Museum, this is Mary, Ellen and Peter from Foxwood School"?' he joked.

'No,' I said patiently. 'I mean I organise activities for the children to do – drawing or painting activities inspired by things in the museum, or questions for them to answer as they go round.'

It wasn't the job I had always wanted, if I was honest. It was usually OK – if you didn't get a group of badly behaved boys running about or hiding somewhere. But it wasn't what I'd hoped to do after I'd left university.

'If you could do anything in the world, what would you do?' asked Leo, and I answered him straight away. I didn't need to think about it.

'I'd travel abroad photographing and writing about beautiful things and places,' I said.

'Are you good at photography?' Leo asked.

'No,' I said, 'not at the moment.'

Leo laughed.

'But I can learn,' I told him.

'This is Big Eye,' Big Eye interrupted us. 'All poems must be completed by ten-thirty. Would Leo please come to the Diary Room?'

Leo looked up towards the ceiling, where the voice seemed to come from. 'Do I have to?' he asked, but Big Eye made no reply. 'I'll take that as a "yes" then,' Leo said, getting up with a sigh.

He was back quickly, carrying lots of clothes in his arms. 'Big Eye wanted me to collect this lot,' he said.

'What is it?' I asked, surprised.

'The clothes we've all got to wear while you read out our poems. Big Eye obviously wants us to look smart.'

I went over to take a look. There were four black suits and a beautiful long dress made out of shiny green material. I touched it. 'How lovely!' I said.

'Lovely for you!' Leo said unhappily. 'I only wear a suit to weddings!'

By eleven o'clock, the men were all dressed in their suits, and I was wearing the long green dress. I had put my hair up too, and I felt good.

'You look lovely, Annie,' Pete said. 'That colour really suits you.'

I smiled at him, thinking what a nice man he was. I'd never heard him say anything unpleasant about anyone, and he was always so helpful. 'Thank you, Pete,' I said. 'And so do you. You *all* do.' It was true – they did. The suits made them all look handsome and ... well, more adult, I suppose.

'This is Big Eye,' Big Eye said. 'The poetry competition will begin in two minutes. Please put all poems in the box on the table. You are reminded that the poems should be anonymous – your name should *not* appear on your poem.'

'Perhaps you should look away, Annie,' Nigel suggested, 'so you don't see us putting our poems into the box.' Nigel always liked to do things properly. He would never break any of Big Eye's rules.

'OK,' I said. 'Good idea.' And I turned away.

'They're all in,' Pete told me after a moment, and I turned back.

'This is Big Eye. The competition will now begin. Annie, please begin reading.'

I stood up and went over to the box. I put my hand inside and pulled out a piece of paper. The writing on it was small and very tidy. I began to read.

'*Annie's eyes are as blue as the sea ...*' I read. Leo laughed loudly and I came to a stop. I looked at him crossly. 'No laughing,' I said, 'or I won't be able to do it.'

'Yes,' said Pete. 'Remember takeaway night!'

'Sorry,' said Leo, still smiling. 'I'll do my best not to laugh.'

Nigel's face was bright red. I thought I knew why – he was the sort of man to have small, tidy writing. I guessed it was his poem.

'I'll begin again,' I said, and gave a little cough to clear my throat.

'Annie's eyes are as blue as the sea;
They make me hope she'll go out with me.
I haven't asked her yet, so until that day,
I hope she'll come to like me in every way.
I want to help her learn to cook,
I want to teach her to enjoy a good book.
We're very different, but here's the thing,
I really want her to wear my ring.'

Leo's shoulders had started to shake halfway through the poem. He had his hand over his mouth, but I could see tears of laughter running down his face. Pete and Simon were smiling too, but Nigel looked completely embarrassed.

'That was, er . . . very nice,' I said, not sure what else to say. At that, Leo couldn't hide his laughter any longer. It exploded out loudly, and Nigel got angrily to his feet.

'Oh, grow up, Leo!' he shouted.

Chapter 3 *Winners and jokes*

Leo tried to stop laughing, but didn't manage it.

'It was a very … nice poem,' I said again, though I hadn't actually liked it at all. The writer, Nigel, didn't seem to be happy with me. He'd wanted to change a lot about me, but he still said he wanted me to wear his ring. I found *that* rather hard to believe.

Nigel was still staring angrily at Leo. 'You never take anything seriously, do you, Leo?' he said.

Leo smiled. 'I try not to,' he said.

'Come on, Nigel,' Pete said gently. 'Sit down, eh? This is only supposed to be a bit of fun.'

Nigel sat down and Pete looked over at me. 'Maybe you ought to move on to the next poem, Annie,' he suggested.

That seemed like a good idea. 'OK,' I said. 'Poem number two.' I gave another little cough before I began.

'She's like a sleepy mouse when she wakes up,
Until she's drunk from her coffee cup.
She has accidents every day,
Falling over things that are in the way.
She uses the wrong words and she drops the tea,
But this crazy girl is the one for me.'

This poem made nearly everyone smile. Even I thought it was quite sweet, and a lot like me. From the look on his face, I thought Pete had written it.

'OK,' I said, taking another piece of paper out of the box. 'Poem number three.' The writing was confident and angry-looking. Without reading a word, I guessed the poem was Simon's.

'Not sporty,
Not forty.
Not too fat,
Thanks for that!
A bad cook,
With a good look.
She's very funny,
Even without the money.
But as it's there,
Why not share?
Ann, Ann, Ann;
I'm your man!'

Leo was laughing again. I didn't want to look at Simon, because I was sure he would have a face like murder, so I moved quickly on.

'Right,' I said. 'The last poem – poem number four.' It was the shortest of all of them.

'She's not boring, she's good fun;
Annie is twenty different women in one.
Likes to laugh, makes mistakes,
Always burns her chocolate cakes!'

We all laughed at that one. The week before it had been Pete's birthday and I'd decided to make him a birthday cake. Unfortunately, I'd forgotten all about it after I'd put it in the oven. It had been a lovely hot day, and we'd all been outside in the pool. None of us had smelt the cake until it was completely black and burnt.

'This is Big Eye. All the poems have been read. Annie should now decide which poem is the best. The prize for the winner will be a date with Annie.'

'That's great!' somebody said – Simon, I think. I wasn't sure because I was busy trying to decide who I wanted to win. I was supposed to decide which poem was best, but it was difficult to keep to that rule. I thought I knew who had written each poem, and the prize was a date with me. I'm only human, after all, so I was trying to decide who I wanted to have a date with.

Not Nigel; I'd gone off him with all his talk about rings and helping me to read books. Didn't he think I had to read books for my job? And as for cooking, *he* wasn't exactly an amazing cook himself. The curry he'd made the other night had been almost too hot to eat. No, not Nigel, which meant not poem number one.

Leo? No, that would be like having a date with my brother. His poem was obviously poem number four, as it was the shortest and Leo had been so quick writing it.

Pete then; poem number two? Well, Pete was nice. My mum would want me to choose Pete, and I *did* like him. But really, there was only one choice – Simon, with his film-star good looks. An evening of him smiling at me across a table would be very enjoyable. So, poem number three it was.

'Will Annie please name the winning poem,' Big Eye ordered me, and I took a deep breath.

'The winner of the poetry competition is ...' I paused, looking at each of the men in turn. Leo had his usual smile on his face, but the others looked as if they cared about the result. I suddenly felt very powerful. 'Poem number three!'

'Yes!' Leo said, throwing his arms into the air.

'What?' I said.

'I told you!' Nigel said angrily, standing up. 'I told you he would win. He's a *writer*! It was always going to be him!'

'For once I agree with you, Nigel,' Simon said, not looking happy. 'The whole competition was a complete waste of time.'

I was confused. I looked at Leo. '*You* wrote poem number three?' I asked, and he nodded.

'I certainly did!' he said, smiling all over his face.

'Well done, Leo,' Pete said, ever the nice guy.

'Leo,' said Big Eye, 'your prize is a date with Annie this evening. You should both go to the Diary Room at eight o'clock. Everyone else should know that no takeaway meal will be provided for them this evening.'

Simon was still looking fed up. 'Do you know what?' he said. 'I'm going to the Diary Room to tell Big Eye exactly what I think about this. It isn't fair.' And off he went.

'And I'm going to have a short sleep,' said Leo, getting up with a yawn. 'Writing poetry makes me very tired.'

'Take your suit off,' Pete advised him. 'You'll need to look smart for your big date tonight.'

Leo nodded and gave me a big smile. 'Can't wait,' he said, and then he went to the bedroom, leaving me with Pete and Nigel.

'Well,' said Pete, 'I think I'd better not give up my engineering job. I'm obviously not a good poet!'

I looked at him. 'They were *all* good,' I said, still feeling disappointed that I wasn't going to be having a date with Simon. Especially as he was so disappointed about losing. He had obviously *wanted* to win a date with me.

Pete laughed. 'I think you ought to read more poetry, Annie, if you think that! Anyone for a cup of tea?'

'All right,' said Nigel sadly. 'I suppose I may as well.'

'Annie?' asked Pete.

I shook my head. 'No thanks, Pete,' I said, still thinking about the competition. I'd been so sure that Simon had written poem number three. I looked through the poems, pulling out poem number three and reading some of it again.

She's very funny, even without the money. But as it's there, why not share? What did Leo mean by that? Was he suggesting we had a romance to win the £10,000? Well, if he was, then he was going to be out of luck!

'Er ... did you like my poem, Annie?' Nigel asked.

I looked up at him. 'Which poem was yours?' I asked, even though I knew.

'Poem number one,' he said. 'I was quite pleased with it myself.' And as he smiled, he *did* look very pleased with himself indeed.

Suddenly I felt extremely angry with him. While I wasn't prepared to pretend to have a romance to win some money, I *was* prepared to make fun of Nigel. Well, it was only fair – he shouldn't have written all that rubbish in his poem.

I put the poems down and went to sit next to him. 'Oh yes, Nigel,' I said softly, looking right into his eyes. 'I *loved* your poem! How *kind* of you to want to help me learn new things!'

Nigel's smile grew. 'I thought you'd like that bit,' he said, not realising at all that I was getting more and more cross with him.

'But,' I said, moving closer and putting my hand on his arm, 'the bit I *really* liked the best was the bit where you said you wanted me to wear your ring!'

'Oh, that bit,' said Nigel, starting to look a bit doubtful.

'Yes!' I said, still staring into his eyes. 'I *loved* that bit. And ... the answer's yes!'

Nigel's face was looking a bit white now. He tried to move away from me, but I pulled his arm to bring him closer again. 'What ... what do you mean?' he asked in a whisper.

'Well,' I explained, 'in that poem you asked me to marry you, didn't you? And the answer's yes!'

I'd never seen a man look so frightened before. His eyes were huge. It was *so* funny. I might just have managed not to explode with laughter though, if Pete hadn't started laughing.

'Can't you see she's joking, Nigel?' he said, coming back with the tea.

And then I let go of Nigel's arm and laughed so much my stomach hurt. 'You looked so worried!' I said to him when I could finally speak again.

Nigel looked at me crossly. 'That's not funny,' he said.

'Oh yes, it is,' Pete said, and that started me off laughing all over again.

'You shouldn't have put it in your poem if you didn't mean it,' I told him after a while.

'I couldn't think of anything else,' Nigel said crossly.

Simon came out of the Diary Room. He looked even more fed up than ever. 'I tried to tell them it wasn't a fair competition,' he told us, 'but they wouldn't say anything.'

'What about the takeaway?' Nigel wanted to know.

Simon shook his head. 'They wouldn't change their minds about that either. No takeaway.'

'Never mind,' Pete said. 'How about a nice cup of tea?'

Simon looked angry. 'That's your answer to everything, isn't it?' he said. 'A nice cup of tea. No thanks.' And with that, he went out into the garden, closing the door noisily after him.

'Now that is one disappointed man,' Pete said, as we all sat and stared after Simon.

Nigel was still cross with me. 'He's disappointed about the takeaway, *not* losing out on a date with Annie,' he said.

'Thanks, Nigel,' I said, getting up and following Simon.

He was sitting on the garden seat. His sunglasses hid his eyes, but his mouth showed how fed up he was. I sat next to him without saying anything for a moment.

Then I said, 'I'm sorry about the takeaway.'

He tried to smile. 'I'm not worried about the takeaway,' he said. 'I'm just a bit fed up with being stuck in here.'

'Are you?' I asked.

'Yes,' he said. 'It's not how I imagined it would be. All the sitting around with nothing to do; all the stupid chat. Sometimes it's like an old people's home in here! I've never been so bored in all my life.'

'Oh,' I said, disappointed that Simon felt that way.

'Look, you're all nice people; it's not that,' Simon went on. 'Especially you, Annie. It's just that I'm the type of person who needs goals to work towards, and I'm not talking about silly music shows or poetry competitions. Maybe it would be best if I was the one to leave next.'

'Well,' I said, my face going red as I spoke, 'I don't want you to leave.'

Simon smiled at me. I wished he wasn't wearing the sunglasses so I could see his eyes.

'It *would* be boring in here without you,' I went on.

Simon took my hand. I felt the electricity from his touch go right up my arm. 'You're very sweet, Annie,' he said. 'Don't listen to me. I'm just feeling sorry for myself.'

He was still holding my hand, and it made me feel brave. 'I'm sorry you didn't win the competition,' I told him. 'I … I wanted you to win.'

'Ah,' Simon said, 'poor Annie. Are you very disappointed your date isn't with me?'

My face was turning even redder. 'Yes, I am,' I said. 'Are … are you?'

Simon's white-toothed smile shone out again. '*Of course* I am,' he said. With his free hand he reached out to touch my hair. His fingers were long and confident. Perfect for making carrot flowers and paper boats. 'Look at you,' he said.

'What?' I asked, putting a hand up to my hair. It wasn't all on top of my head any more – most of it had dropped down around my shoulders. I must look a real mess. If only I had my comb.

'Funny, messy Annie,' Simon said softly. 'How nice it would be to have a date with you! But we'll just have to do something special together another time, won't we?'

Soon after that Simon decided he was going to do some more jogging. I watched him for a while, and then I walked dreamily back indoors. Maybe there would be a romance in the House after all – a romance between Simon and me!

Chapter 4 *Messy spaghetti*

At exactly eight o'clock, Leo and I went to the Diary Room together. Leo was still wearing his suit, and he still looked smart. Well, almost smart – his tie wasn't quite straight. As for me, I'm afraid I didn't look quite as smart as I had in the morning. At lunchtime we'd had soup and some had got on my dress. Although I'd done my best to clean it off, you could still see where it had been. Soup and I just didn't go together. I wished I'd changed out of the dress.

'Do you think we're going to have our date in the Diary Room?' Leo asked, and I looked at him, surprised.

'No!' I said, but actually I hadn't thought about it. 'You don't think so, do you?'

'Well,' said Leo, 'dates are supposed to be private, aren't they? And the Diary Room, the toilets and the shower are the only private places, aren't they?' He smiled down at me. 'Got your soap?'

'Good evening, Annie. Good evening, Leo,' said Big Eye. It was a woman this time.

'Hi there, Big Eye,' said Leo.

'Hello, Big Eye,' I said, and for some strange reason I suddenly felt a bit nervous. I couldn't imagine why – this was only Leo, after all. Now, if it had been *Simon* I was waiting to have a date with, *then* I would have had a good reason to feel nervous.

'Your date this evening will be a meal for two,' Big Eye told us. I half-expected Leo to make a joke about eating dinner in the shower, but he didn't.

'If you press the button on the wall behind the chair, a door will open,' Big Eye told us. 'Go through, and you will find your table waiting for you.'

Leo and I looked at each other, smiling. A secret door – how exciting!

'Thank you, Big Eye,' I said.

Leo was already reaching behind the chair.

'Got it!' he said, and next moment the wall was opening up and he was walking through to the room on the other side. 'Come on, Annie!' he said, and I quickly followed him. It felt like a real adventure.

'Oh!' I said as I got inside. '*Oh!*'

The room was beautiful. It was small, and it was painted a pinkish red colour. The table was covered in a beautiful tablecloth made of shiny red material, and it was laid with shining silver knives and forks. But it was the lights that took my breath away as I went in. They were everywhere you looked – tiny silver-white lights that made the room look warm. It was extremely romantic.

Leo was holding out one of the chairs for me. 'Do sit down,' he said with a smile.

I laughed. 'Thank you, kind sir,' I said.

Leo went round to the other side of the table and sat down himself. As he did, the secret door closed.

'We're shut in,' I said.

Leo looked up at the cameras on the wall. 'Just you, me and a million or two viewers then,' he joked.

'I wonder how we're going to get our food?' I asked.

'Good question,' said Leo, but at that moment Big Eye spoke.

'Welcome to the Big Eye Restaurant,' she said.

I caught Leo's eye – he had a big smile on his face – and I had to put a hand over my mouth to stop myself from laughing.

'Your first course is ready,' Big Eye told us. 'Press the button under the table and a door will open.'

'They like their buttons here, don't they?' Leo said, bending down to have a look.

'Let me press it this time!' I said, and quickly bent down to look under the table. 'Where is it?' And I began feeling around under the table. It was difficult to see, because I had the tablecloth in my eyes. I pushed it out of the way and saw Leo smiling at me under the table.

'You look different upside down,' he said.

'You don't,' I laughed. 'You look about the same.'

'Thanks!' he said. 'And the button's there, I think.'

I saw where he was pointing. 'Oh yes,' I said, and reached out to press it. Immediately there was a noise from somewhere above, and I quickly moved my head to see what was happening. Unfortunately I moved a bit too quickly and managed to hit my head on the table.

'Ow!' I said, holding my head.

'Are you OK?' asked Leo.

'Yes, yes,' I said impatiently. 'Look, over there!'

A small door had opened, showing a hole in the wall. In it were two bowls.

'Allow me,' said Leo, who was clearly on his best behaviour this evening. He went over to the hole in the wall and came back with two bowls of delicious-looking fruit.

'I'm pleased it isn't soup,' I said.

Leo smiled. 'Big Eye wouldn't be that horrible to you twice in a day,' he said.

'Wouldn't he?' I said, picking up a piece of fruit.

'She, tonight,' Leo said.

'Oh yes,' I said. 'Sorry, she. What *is* this fruit? I asked. 'Do you know?'

'No idea,' Leo said. 'Something unusual. It smells nice though.'

I put the fruit in my mouth and took a bite. Immediately juice from the fruit ran right down my arm. 'Oh!' I said, and Leo laughed. 'Why didn't that happen to you?' I asked.

He shook his head. 'I don't know, Annie,' he said. 'It's one of the unexplained facts of life. Annie Tyler equals mess and accidents.'

'I'm not completely hopeless,' I said, trying to get the juice off my arm with a handkerchief and starting to feel a bit annoyed.

'Of course not,' Leo agreed. 'You're not sporty, not forty. Not too fat ...'

'OK, OK,' I interrupted him. 'Thank you. Anyway, what does Leo Brown equal? If I'm mess and accidents, what are you?'

'You tell me,' Leo said, taking a large bite of his fruit. 'What do you think Leo Brown equals?'

'Joking and sleeping,' I said, without having to think about it. 'Leo Brown equals joking and sleeping.'

'That's in *here*,' Leo told me. 'But that's not the real Leo Brown.'

'So what is the "real" Leo Brown like?' I asked, attempting another bite of fruit.

'Well, he thinks a lot, and after he's thought, he actually works very hard. When he's not meeting up with his friends and being sociable.'

'You think a lot here too,' I told him.

'Do I?' asked Leo.

I nodded. 'Yes. Oh, you chat and you make your jokes, but you watch us too. And you listen to what we say very carefully. Sometimes I think we'll all end up as characters in one of your books.'

Leo shook his head. 'Before I came to the Big Eye House, I had to promise that I wouldn't use anything that happens here in my future writing. That includes any of the people I meet in here. So don't worry; you're safe. You won't pick up one of my books in an airport and discover I've made you a murderer in it.'

'I wouldn't be a very believable murderer anyway,' I told him. 'Not with all the mistakes I make.'

'What's the worst mistake you've ever made?' Leo asked. 'Your most embarrassing moment.'

I thought about it. There were so many to choose from. 'Well,' I said, 'there was the time when my bikini top fell off when I jumped into the swimming pool. And the time I was working in a hospital when I was a student. I had to give patients their meals in their beds and I dropped a big bowl of peas on the floor. They went under everyone's beds.'

Leo began to laugh. I didn't mind; it was funny now, looking back on it. It had taken ages to find all the peas.

'And it wasn't a very good moment when I locked two schoolboys in one of the rooms in the museum,' I continued.

'Did you *intend* to lock them in?' Leo asked.

'No!' I said impatiently. 'Of course I didn't. I had no idea they were in there. They were hiding from their teacher for a joke. I thought everyone had come out of the room, so I locked up. It's a room that people can only go into with someone from the museum.'

'Were they in there all night?' Leo wanted to know.

'No,' I said. 'Only ten minutes or so. But I had turned the lights off, so it was quite dark, and there were some Egyptian bodies in there – you know, mummies.'

Leo laughed. 'I imagine those boys will never run off to hide again,' he said.

'They may never even visit a museum again,' I said. 'They were really afraid. And the teacher was very angry about it. I got into big trouble with my boss.'

'Poor Annie,' Leo said.

'I do get tired of people thinking I'm hopeless all the time. I said. 'It would be nice to be taken seriously.'

Leo looked at me. 'You have fruit juice on the end of your nose,' he said.

I reached crossly for my – now very wet – handkerchief. 'You see?' I said, using it on my nose. 'There's absolutely no hope of anyone ever taking me seriously, is there?'

There was a sound at the hole in the wall. Leo and I both looked up at the same time and saw – two large plates of very messy spaghetti bolognese.

'Oh, no!' I said. 'I'm useless at eating spaghetti!' Then I looked at Leo and we both began to laugh.

'OK,' he said, collecting up our fruit bowls. 'I've got a suggestion.'

'What?' I asked.

'Well,' Leo said, going over to collect the spaghetti, 'Big Eye has obviously given us spaghetti to eat for a reason.'

'Yes,' I said, 'to make me look as stupid as possible!'

'My suggestion is that we *both* look stupid. We both make as much mess as possible. We don't even try to keep our clothes clean. If Big Eye wants mess, let's give her mess!'

I smiled at him. 'You're crazy,' I told him. 'Do you know that?'

'Plenty of past girlfriends have told me so,' he said. He put one of the plates of spaghetti on the table in front of me. 'But I also like to think I'm fun. So what do you say? Shall we have a bit of messy fun?'

It was going to happen anyway with me eating spaghetti. It might as well be planned. 'OK then,' I said. 'Let's do it!'

'Right,' said Leo, lifting his fork. 'One, two, three, go!'

Chapter 5 *Leaving Night*

By the end of our meal, my face was red with bolognese sauce and Leo had spaghetti in his hair. There was spaghetti everywhere and we had laughed so much I was exhausted. It was like being five years old all over again.

I smiled at Leo across the table. 'Thanks,' I said.

'What for?' he asked.

'Well,' I said, 'for making this fun. It would have been awful to eat that meal with someone who was embarrassed about me making a mess.'

Leo looked at me. 'And which of the other guys would have been embarrassed, do you think?'

I thought about it. 'Nigel, probably. Yes, definitely Nigel. He would have been so embarrassed about it, the whole meal would have been silent.'

'Except for the sound of you eating spaghetti?' Leo smiled.

'Yes,' I agreed, 'except for that.'

'Who else would have been embarrassed, do you think?'

I thought about it again. 'Pete, probably,' I said. 'But he would be far too nice to mention it.'

'Pleasant Pete,' Leo said, and I smiled.

'He *is* Pleasant Pete,' I said.

Leo looked at me. 'What about Simon?' he asked. 'If Pete is Pleasant Pete, what's Simon?'

I played with the spaghetti I had left on my plate with my fork. *Sexy* Simon, I thought, but I didn't say that. 'Sporty Simon?' I suggested instead.

'And me?' Leo asked.

I looked at him, giving it some thought. 'Laughing Leo,' I said. 'Definitely. And sometimes – especially when we need someone to wash up the dirty plates – Lazy Leo.'

Leo smiled at me. 'Don't be Awful Annie,' he joked, and I laughed.

'Very funny,' I said.

Then suddenly Leo's face became more serious. 'You know Simon would have been embarrassed by your spaghetti eating too, don't you?'

I looked at him, feeling confused. 'Well,' I said, 'I don't think he would.'

'Of course he would,' Leo said.

'He would not!' I argued.

'You just think he's so great you don't want to think anything bad about him,' Leo told me.

'That's not true,' I said. 'I know Simon, that's all. He wouldn't be like that. He's a really nice man, and he likes me.'

Leo looked annoyed. 'Why are you girls always so blind when it comes to good looks?' he asked. 'Anyone can see that the man is only interested in himself! He's completely selfish.'

'Simon was very disappointed he wasn't coming on this date!' I said angrily.

'I expect he was,' Leo said. 'But that doesn't mean anything. The man has no heart. He's as thin as … I don't know, a piece of paper.'

'Simon isn't ...' I began, but Leo interrupted me.

'Oh, I don't mean *physically* thin,' Leo said. 'The man's body is perfect, I'm sure. It's his brain that worries me – his brain and his heart. In my opinion, they're both rather empty.'

'Well,' I said, 'I disagree completely.'

'That's OK,' said Leo. 'You're allowed to disagree.' He paused, and then looked at me. 'I'm right though; you'll see.'

Things were difficult between us after this conversation. I was quite pleased when the secret door to the room opened again and the date was over.

Pete laughed when Leo and I came out of the Diary Room. 'Have you two had a food fight?' he asked.

I put a hand up to my tomato-red face. I'd been so busy being cross with Leo, I'd forgotten all about the messy spaghetti.

'In a way,' answered Leo, looking at me.

'Did Big Eye forget to provide knives and forks?' Simon asked, looking at my red face.

Straight away my face went even redder. I avoided looking at Leo. 'Leo and I just had a bit of fun,' I said.

'It doesn't look like much fun to me,' Nigel said. 'That spaghetti will make a lot of mess in the shower.'

Leo began to laugh. 'We'll see, shall we?' he said, and he walked off towards the bathroom.

'That's not very polite,' Pete said. 'He didn't ask you if you wanted to use the shower first, Annie.'

'Leo's *not* a lot of things,' Simon said. 'He's not polite, he's not active, he's not a good cook, he's not funny ...'

'Oh, Simon,' Pete said, 'I just can't agree with you there. Leo's definitely funny.'

Yes, I thought. He is funny. Very funny. And suddenly I felt … well, a bit sad. It had been a really nice evening until Leo and I had argued. I wished we hadn't.

'Well,' Simon was saying. 'It's Leaving Night tomorrow – someone's going to go. We'll see what the public thinks, won't we? If they agree with me that Leo isn't funny, that he's just *annoying*, then he'll be leaving the House.'

* * *

We were always nervous on Leaving Night, although we all tried to hide it in different ways. Simon was normally out jogging right up until Big Eye told him to sit on the sofa. That's where we had to be to hear the result of the vote. The rest of us sat about and laughed – usually about something Leo had said. We pretended we didn't have a care in the world, when in fact we were all worried. None of us wanted to leave the House.

This Leaving Night was different. Leo had been quieter than usual all day, and things were still a bit difficult between him and me. Nigel was still looking bad-tempered with me, I thought, so he wasn't saying very much. Pete was the only person in a good mood, but even he had run out of things to say. So we were a very quiet – and probably very boring – group as we waited to be told who was to leave.

It was a warm night, and the doors to the garden were open. Every Leaving Night there was a large crowd of people outside. They came to see the person who was told to leave the House, and it was always noisy. That night it was *very* noisy indeed. We could hear people shouting, but we couldn't hear what they were shouting about.

It was very strange, sitting there on the sofas, waiting to see if you would be the one chosen to go. You thought about walking out there in front of all those shouting people. You thought about all the cameras pointing at you, and all the questions you'd be asked. Waiting for the result of the vote was like waiting for an exam result.

On Leaving Nights I also always thought about my family and friends and my life outside the House. I missed them, so every time I wasn't chosen to leave I felt a bit sad. Even though I was happy to be staying. I expect that sounds a bit crazy, but it's difficult to describe exactly what it was like.

That Leaving Night, I was trying not to think about anything. But it's hard to think about nothing, so I thought about the present I'd received that morning instead. Yes, another present – a smiling face made out of a round piece of soap! Very simple, but it had made me smile.

Nigel hadn't been smiling though. He'd come into the kitchen wearing only a towel. 'Who's hidden the soap?' he'd asked crossly.

So, I thought, it's not you leaving me presents.

Nigel still looked cross as we waited that evening on the sofas for Violet Carlton to speak to us. We all knew she was outside the House in the crowd. We would know who was leaving any minute.

I looked up and saw that Simon was looking at me. 'I hope you don't go, Annie,' he said with a smile.

'It might be *you* going,' Leo told him.

'Don't start arguing again, you two,' Pete began to say, but at that moment Violet Carlton spoke to us.

'Big Eye House,' she said, 'this is Violet.' The sound of the crowd outside was very loud. Violet almost had to shout for us to hear her. 'The votes have been counted. The public has made a decision. The person who will be leaving the Big Eye House tonight is ...' Violet always paused before she told us the name. It made it more exciting for the people watching the TV programme. '... Nigel!'

We all looked at Nigel. He smiled, but his face was red.

'Nigel,' Violet said, 'you have five minutes to say goodbye to everybody and to pack your bag.'

Nigel got to his feet. We all looked at him. 'It's all right,' he said, before we could say anything. 'I'm happy to go. I've had enough of this place!' And he went off to the bedroom to pack his suitcase. Five minutes later, he was gone.

'So,' said Pete with a smile. 'Now there are only four of us.'

Nobody answered. We were too busy listening to the shouts of the crowd as the doors opened and Nigel walked out.

Chapter 6 *Food and jumping*

'Big Eye would like you to decide on a task for the three men who are left, Annie,' Big Eye told me. It was a man this time. 'Once again, it should be something to show how they feel about you.'

I'd been in the pool when Big Eye had called me into the Diary Room. So now I was sitting in my swimsuit, making the chair wet.

I didn't want the men to have to do another task about me. But I knew Big Eye wouldn't change his mind, so I didn't complain. Instead, I sat there and thought about what I could suggest.

That morning I'd received another present. It had been a plate of fruit, probably arranged in the shape of a face or something. But unfortunately it had fallen onto the floor when I woke up, so I wasn't sure. I still wanted to know who was leaving the presents for me. Maybe I could choose a task that would help me to find out who it was.

'OK,' I said to Big Eye. 'I've got an idea for a task.'

'Would you like to tell me your idea, Annie?' Big Eye asked.

'I'd like them to make something for me,' I said. 'I don't mind what it is – they can make what they like. But it should be a thoughtful gift – something they think I'd really like.'

There was a pause. I waited, imagining the different Big Eyes discussing my idea.

'Big Eye accepts your idea for today's task, Annie,' Big Eye said at last. 'Please go and tell the men what they have to do. They have two hours before they have to present their gifts to you. While they are preparing their gifts, you should wait in the bedroom.'

Great – two boring hours on my own in the bedroom. Still, it would be worth it if I discovered who was leaving me the presents.

* * *

'What sort of thing do you want us to make?' Simon wanted to know after I'd told them about the task.

'That's your decision,' I told him. 'Big Eye wants it to be something that will show how you feel about me. I think you should try to think of something I need or something you know I would like.'

Simon and Pete looked thoughtful. Leo was smiling. 'Have you already got an idea?' I asked him.

His smile grew. 'Perhaps,' he said.

'This is Big Eye,' Big Eye said. 'Today's task will now begin. Annie, please go to the bedroom.'

'Good luck!' I said and I went off, wondering if my plan would work. I really wanted to find out who was leaving me the presents.

* * *

At one o'clock, Big Eye told me to go into the living area. When I got there, I found that only Pete was there. I could see the others outside, in the pool. Leo saw me and gave me a wave through the window.

'What's going on?' I asked Pete.

He smiled at me. 'Big Eye has asked me to present my gift first,' he said.

I smiled back at him, looking around the room. 'Right,' I said. 'Where is it then?'

'Over here,' Pete said. 'If you'd like to come this way?' Pete led me to the dining table, where I saw two – very large – plates of food waiting for us. 'I decided to make you lunch,' Pete told me. 'My mum has always said that the way to someone's heart is through their stomach!'

'Yes,' I said, not knowing *what* to say. To tell the truth, I wasn't feeling very hungry. It was a hot day, and Pete had cooked meat, potatoes and vegetables. I would have preferred a salad. 'My grandmother used to say that too,' I said.

'Well,' Pete said, still with that big smile, 'let's hope it's true!'

I sat down in front of one of the plates of food. Did Pete really want to find the way to my heart? Did he really want me to like him in that way – as a girlfriend? He hadn't given me any sign of it before. He'd always been very nice to me, but he was nice to everyone. He was like a friend, not a boyfriend. Maybe he was one of those men who can't show how they feel very easily.

'This looks ... lovely,' I said bravely, picking up my knife and fork. 'Have you always enjoyed cooking?'

'Oh yes,' Pete said, and he began to tell me all about how he had learnt to cook, what he liked cooking best, his cooking mistakes ... I listened, nodding every now and then as I chewed my food. Every time he stopped speaking, I asked him another question to get him to start talking again. I suppose I wanted to take his attention away from me, because I knew I definitely didn't want him to think of me as a girlfriend. I just didn't feel that way about him, and I didn't want him to be the person who was leaving me the presents.

After I had eaten as much as I could – which was just under half of the food on the plate – I smiled at Pete.

'Thanks so much, Pete,' I said. 'That was delicious. But perhaps I'd better go and see what Simon and Leo have made for me now.'

'But the meal isn't over yet!' Pete said, jumping up. He went over to the freezer and came back with two very large bowls of ice cream.

By the time I finally went out into the garden, I was feeling a bit sick.

'Hello, Annie!' Simon said, getting out of the pool. 'Ready for my gift?'

'She looks as if she needs a rest first,' Leo laughed.

'Of course she doesn't need a rest!' Simon said, drying himself with a towel.

At any other time I'm sure I would have enjoyed watching Simon drying himself, but not then. 'Well, actually ...' I began, but Simon was already throwing the towel down and walking towards me.

'Come on,' he said, taking my arm. 'We've got work to do.'

He wasn't joking. Simon's gift to me was a physical training plan. 'You're not fat, of course,' he said, 'but everybody needs to keep their body in good condition. Just do what I do.' And Simon began to jump and to run and to stretch. I did my best to follow what he was doing, but it was hot, and my stomach was full of food. Simon did everything very quickly as well. He was always moving on to a jump before I had finished a stretch, or to a stretch before I had finished a jump.

'I'm sorry, Simon,' I kept on saying.

'That's all right,' he said. 'You're doing fine.'

But I wasn't, and Leo clearly found it all very amusing. He was sitting on the edge of the pool smiling, and – when I actually fell over once – laughing. I was starting to get really angry with him. Simon was obviously getting angry with him as well, because suddenly he stopped jumping and reached out to push Leo into the pool.

But Leo found this even more amusing – he was still laughing when his head came out of the water.

'Everything's a joke to you, isn't it?' Simon said angrily.

But Leo couldn't speak. He was laughing too much.

I thought Simon might jump into the pool to hit him, but instead he looked at me. 'Well,' he said, 'that's my gift to you, Annie. If you do that every day your body will soon be in excellent condition.'

I was so tired I could hardly speak. 'Oh,' I said. 'Thank you. Thank you very much, Simon.'

'Don't mention it,' Simon said politely. 'Right, if you'll excuse me, Annie, I'll go inside for a shower now. If I stay out here any longer, I might do something to shut Leo up for ever.'

I watched him walk off, and then I sat down in a garden chair. Leo was still laughing.

'Shut up, Leo!' I said with my eyes closed.

I heard him come and sit in the chair next to me. 'I'm sorry,' he said, 'but you have no idea how funny that was!'

'Oh,' I said weakly, 'I think I do. And if your gift is anything to do with food or physical improvement, then you can forget it!'

'My gift is about improving your mind,' he told me.

'Improving my mind?' I repeated tiredly. 'What *can* you have made for me?'

'I've made you a questionnaire,' Leo said. 'A list of questions for you to think about and answer.'

I looked at him. 'Questions about what?' I asked.

Leo smiled. 'About you,' he said.

'Me?' I asked.

He nodded. 'Yes,' he said. 'They're designed to make you think about what you want from life, and exactly how happy you are at the moment.'

'And this questionnaire is something you think I would want, is it?' I asked him.

'You said the gift should be something you would like or something we thought you needed,' he reminded me.

I was fed up. Pete had thought I needed food, Simon had thought I needed to work on my body, and now Leo thought I needed to work on my mind. Nobody seemed to be happy with me just as I was. And I still had no idea who was leaving me the presents.

'Go on then,' I said unhappily to Leo. 'Show me this questionnaire of yours. I'll try to answer your questions.'

Chapter 7 *Questions, questions*

In the end, Leo read the questions out to me.

'Right,' he said. 'Question number one. If you had one year left to live, what would you do?'

'That's a difficult one!' I said.

'They're all difficult,' Leo told me cheerfully.

'Oh, I don't know,' I said. 'Give up my job? Travel the world? Does anybody know what they'd do unless it actually happened?'

'Question number two,' Leo went on. 'What three things do you think you *must* do before you die?'

'Are all the questions about death?' I asked him.

'Not all of them, no,' he said. 'Come on, three things.'

'All right,' I said. 'Let's see.' Actually, it wasn't a difficult question to answer. I just felt a bit silly sharing my very private secrets with everybody. 'I'd travel the world, I'd have a child with the man of my dreams and I'd buy a house.'

'In that order?' Leo asked.

'Well,' I said, 'I suppose it would be best if the house came before the child.'

'And the man of your dreams came before the child?' Leo joked.

'Very funny,' I said. 'Come on, next question.'

Leo looked down at his piece of paper. 'OK,' he said, 'now we move on to your job. Question number three is what's the worst thing about your job and question number four is what's the best thing about it?'

'Well,' I said, 'I suppose the worst thing is that it's quite similar every day. The same old routines week after week. And the best thing …' I paused, realising that my boss might be watching the programme. Or, if he wasn't, then somebody else who worked at the museum probably was.

'Come on,' Leo said. 'Tell the truth.'

'OK,' I said. 'I suppose the best thing about my job is getting my salary paid into my bank at the end of every month.' I looked at Leo. 'That's not very good, is it?'

'Well,' said Leo, 'it moves us on nicely to question number five – if your dream job would be to travel the world photographing and writing about beautiful things and places, then why aren't you doing it?'

'Because I can't afford it, I suppose,' I said. 'Or I'm just not brave enough or ambitious enough to take the first step. I don't know.'

Leo looked at me. I expected him to say something about my answer, but he didn't. 'OK, question number six,' he said instead. 'When are you going to take a photography course?'

I had intended to start one the year before, *and* the year before that. But I hadn't. 'In the autumn, I expect,' I said. 'Honestly, Leo, do you know how fed up this questionnaire of yours is making me? I feel like a complete failure.'

Leo didn't seem to care. 'It's all for your own good,' he told me. 'Right; this is the final question.' He paused, looking at me.

I was feeling annoyed with him by now. Why did he feel it was his job to make me think about all this stuff? OK, so I probably did need to think about it; no, I *definitely* needed to think about it. I was at a crossroads in my life and I needed to make some decisions. But I didn't need to do it in front of millions of television viewers.

'What sort of man do you think would be the perfect boyfriend for you?'

I smiled. It was nice not to have to think about my job any more. 'Oh,' I said, 'that's easy. My perfect boyfriend would be a kind man. Someone who enjoys life, but who really cares about what he does. Someone who enjoys doing the same kind of things I do.'

'So,' Leo asked, 'he doesn't have to be good-looking then?'

'Well ...' I said, 'no, but I'd need to find him attractive.'

Leo laughed. I looked at him. 'I don't see why that's funny,' I said.

'It's not,' he said. 'You're just being honest.'

'You wanted me to be honest, didn't you?' I said. 'And anyway, I'm sure you haven't had any girlfriends you didn't find attractive.'

'Of course not,' Leo said.

'Well then!' I said.

'But they weren't all perfect either,' Leo said. 'Sometimes I find the way someone laughs attractive. Or the way they smile. The way they love life. There just has to be *something*, that's all.'

I looked at Leo crossly. 'First it was careers advice, and now it's relationship advice. And yet you're single, aren't you?'

'Yes,' said Leo.

'And you've been single for some time?'

'Yes,' said Leo.

'So you don't know everything then, do you?' I asked. 'If you did, you'd be attached by now.'

'I never said I did know everything,' Leo said.

I looked at him. 'You always have to have the last word, don't you?' I said. 'You *have* to win an argument.'

'Are we having an argument?' Leo asked.

My head was starting to hurt. 'Go away, Leo,' I said, and closed my eyes.

There was the sound of paper moving about. 'I was going anyway,' Leo said.

'Good,' I said, and when I opened my eyes next, I was alone. The questionnaire was on the chair next to me.

Immediately I felt guilty about being bad-tempered with Leo. It wasn't his fault that his questions had made me feel bad. I felt bad because I wasn't completely happy with my life at that moment, and his questions reminded me of that. I felt stuck, but I couldn't seem to do anything about it. That's why I'd wanted to come on this show – to do something – anything – different. And it certainly *was* different.

'Hi.' I looked up at the kind voice and smiled. Pete was standing next to me. 'Mind if I join you? If you'd rather be alone, just say.'

I did want to be alone, but I couldn't say so. Pete was just trying to be nice, and I didn't want to hurt him as well as Leo. 'No,' I said, 'that's OK.'

'Are you feeling tired after your day?' he asked.

I smiled again. 'Yes!' I said. 'I certainly am. My head hurts. And my legs.'

'What about your stomach?' Pete asked.

'Well,' I said, 'I don't want to eat anything else until tomorrow! I'm very full.'

Pete laughed. 'Sorry,' he said. 'I did cook a lot of food, didn't I?'

'Enough for about six,' I said.

'I come from a large family,' Pete told me. 'I'm used to cooking big meals.'

'It was a lovely meal, Pete,' I told him. 'And it was a great idea for a present.'

I smiled, and we sat in silence for a while. Somewhere a bird was singing. It was quite peaceful, and I felt myself begin to relax. I closed my eyes to do a bit of sunbathing.

'I wonder what the next task will be?' Pete said.

'I don't want to think about it!' I said, still with my eyes closed.

'Tomorrow evening there'll only be three people here,' Pete said.

'Oh yes,' I said. 'I'd forgotten about that. There's another Leaving Night tomorrow.'

'Yes,' Pete said. 'But none of us has much longer in here. We'll all be returning to our normal lives soon.'

I didn't want to go back to my normal life. Leo's questions had made me recognise how unhappy I was with everything. The question was: what was I going to do about it?

'Well,' I said, making an effort to be cheerful, 'I hope it's not you who goes.'

Pete looked at me. 'Really?' he said. 'You'd prefer it to be one of the others?'

I opened my eyes, thinking about it. I definitely didn't want it to be Simon who left. And as for Leo … I wasn't sure about Leo. He could make me feel tired, but did I really want him to leave? Actually, for some strange reason, I didn't.

I smiled at Pete. 'I don't want any of you to go,' I said.

'One of us will have to,' he said.

'That's true,' I agreed. I looked at him, thinking again what a nice man he was. 'You really like what you do, don't you?' I asked.

'Being an engineer?' Pete said. 'Yes, I love it.'

'What do you like best about it?' I asked, thinking of Leo's questionnaire.

Pete didn't need to think about it. 'I like seeing what I've helped to make, after it's finished,' he told me. 'A bridge or a building – you stand and look at it and you think, I helped to make that. It's a good feeling.'

'It must be,' I said.

We were quiet for a while. I imagined Pete standing there looking at one of his buildings with a big smile on his face. I certainly never smiled like that after a group of schoolchildren left the museum these days. I had when I'd first started the job, I supposed.

'You don't ever get bored with building bridges then?' I asked Pete.

'No,' he said. 'Every bridge is different.'

'That's great,' I said. 'You're very lucky.'

Pete paused for a moment, then he asked, 'Would you like to come and see one of my bridges after this is all finished?'

'I'd love to …' I started to say, but then I turned and looked into his face. There was something about the way he was looking at me which made me wish I hadn't answered so quickly.

Pete reached out to touch my hair. Suddenly, his face seemed very close to mine. 'I'd like to think we could spend some time together after this is over, Annie,' he said. 'Lots of time …'

I was completely surprised by Pete's change of mood, and while I tried to think of something to say, his face was getting closer and closer. *He was going to kiss me!*

Suddenly I jumped to my feet. 'Sorry, Pete!' I said quickly. 'I've got to … to … use the bathroom.' And I ran indoors.

Chapter 8 *Kisses*

'Big Eye House, this is Violet,' Violet Carlton told us the following evening. 'The person who will be leaving the Big Eye house tonight is ...'

Over on the other sofa, Pete avoided my eyes. He'd been doing that most of the day. Neither of us had spoken about what had happened in the garden. Leo and Simon had been around, and there hadn't been a chance for Pete and me to be alone. But that morning, as I made my way to the bathroom, we had met face-to-face.

'Pete,' I had said, 'about yesterday ...'

'Forget it,' he had told me quickly. 'I was silly to think you'd be interested in being my girlfriend.' And with that he'd walked away, leaving me wondering if I was to blame in any way. I didn't think I'd done anything to make Pete believe I found him attractive. I'd told him I hoped he wouldn't be leaving the House, but I'd just been making conversation. Oh dear, perhaps it was my fault.

'... Pete,' Violet Carlton finished.

'Of course,' Pete said, and stood up. Leo and Simon went over to him to shake his hand. I stood up too, but I didn't go over. I wasn't sure if Pete would want me to. I was sorry Pete was leaving. He was a very nice man, and, although I didn't want him to be my boyfriend, I did like him.

'Bad luck,' Leo said.

'That's OK,' Pete said. 'It was always going to be me next. You two are strong, attractive characters – you were never going to be voted out until the end.'

'What about me?' I said, and finally Pete looked over at me.

'Oh no, Annie,' he said. 'It couldn't be you. The public want to keep you here. They want to see a romance.' He came over to me and took hold of my arms, looking down into my face. 'And anyway, you're pretty, funny, caring ...' He paused to smile at me. 'The list goes on. Anyone who *does* have a romance with you will be a very lucky guy – in here or in the outside world.' And while I was busy taking all of this in, Pete kissed me.

Five minutes later, his bag was packed, and he was waiting for the doors to open.

'Pete,' said Violet Carlton, 'you must now leave the Big Eye House.'

The doors began to open. Pete picked up his bag and then looked at Simon and Leo seriously. 'You'd better make sure you're good to Annie,' he told them. 'I'll be watching you.'

Then he walked through the doors. They closed after him. Simon, Leo and I stood there, waiting for the screams and shouts to begin when the outside doors to the building opened. There were stairs outside our exit – when you left the House you had to walk up the stairs and then other doors opened to let you outside.

Suddenly the noise from the people waiting outside started up – a big wall of sound. It didn't matter how often I heard it, it still always came as a surprise.

'Goodbye, Pete,' I said softly.

Beside me, Leo yawned and gave a big stretch. 'Leaving Night makes me very tired,' he said. 'I think I'll have a rest.' And off he went, leaving me alone with Simon.

Simon sat down on one of the sofas. I went to join him. 'That man needs to see a doctor,' he said.

I looked at him. 'Who? Pete?' I asked.

'No, Leo,' Simon said. 'He's always having to have a sleep. Though now I come to think of it, Pete should probably go and see a doctor too. He's clearly feeling very sick. Very *love*sick.'

'Stop it,' I said. 'I feel as if I'm to blame somehow. And yet I don't think I did anything to make him believe I felt that way about him. But I still feel guilty.'

'Don't,' Simon advised me. 'You can't help being pretty, funny and caring, can you? It's not your fault if people fall for you.' He looked at me and took my hand in his. 'He was right about all those things, by the way.'

I felt suddenly hot and looked down at my hand in his. 'Oh,' I said. 'Do you really think so?'

'Yes,' Simon said, 'I do. Although I think he left one important thing off his list. You're also very sexy. Especially with bolognese sauce on your face.'

I looked up at him. 'You're laughing at me,' I said.

Simon smiled. 'Only a little,' he said. 'And only because I like you. I'm very, very happy that out of all the women you're the last one in the House.'

I didn't know what to say. I felt happy and embarrassed all at the same time. 'That's very nice of you, Simon,' I said.

'I'm not saying it to be nice,' Simon told me. 'I'm saying it because it's how I feel.'

I didn't know what to say. Simon hadn't paid me this amount of attention before. It was making me nervous to have him sitting so close to me, looking right into my eyes. He was a very attractive man, and I was feeling the effects of having him so near me. It was a bit like being hit by a train.

'Er ... thank you,' I said nervously, looking at his mouth and wondering if he were going to kiss me in front of millions of viewers. Pete had kissed me, it was true, but that had been different. That had been a goodbye kiss, but this would be ... well, to be honest, I wasn't sure. A 'hello' kiss? The start of a relationship?

The silence stretched on. The moment probably only lasted a few seconds in reality. But sitting there, with Simon looking down at me like that, it felt as if it lasted for *years.* I had to say something, *do* something, or my heart would stop.

I opened my mouth to speak. I had no idea what I was going to say. 'We'd ... we'd better start making dinner, I ... I suppose,' I said.

Simon looked at me. It obviously wasn't what he'd expected to hear. 'Funny little Annie,' he laughed softly. 'Thinking about food at a time like this.'

A door opened somewhere behind us. 'Did someone mention food?' asked Leo in a bright voice. 'I am *so* hungry. What are you going to cook, Annie?'

* * *

'And how are you feeling this evening, Annie?'

I'd been in the Diary Room for about twenty minutes. I'd come to have a bit of time to myself. I know that probably sounds crazy, but it was Simon and Leo I wanted to get away from, not Big Eye or the people watching on TV.

What would have happened if Leo hadn't come into the living area talking about dinner and being hungry? Would Simon have kissed me? Did I want him to kiss me? I'd liked the look of Simon from the first moment I saw him. Of course I wanted him to kiss me. Didn't I?

'I'm feeling ... confused,' I told Big Eye.

'Why is that, Annie?' Big Eye asked. Big Eye was a woman that night. 'I'm not sure what I think about anything,' I told her. 'Everything's mixed up in my mind.' I felt a bit sad, and I could tell it showed in my voice. 'I've realised I'm not happy with my life outside here, but I'm not sure what to do about it. I don't feel ready to leave here yet. Does that sound stupid?'

'Do you think it sounds stupid, Annie?' asked Big Eye. I'd forgotten that Big Eye never, ever gave opinions.

'A bit, yes,' I said. 'But I can't help it. That's the way I feel. And it's not helping having Simon and Leo arguing all the time.'

'Why do you think they're arguing, Annie?' Big Eye asked.

'I suppose they're very different,' I said. 'And they're both people who think they're always right.'

This was followed by one of Big Eye's pauses. I wondered if Simon and Leo were still arguing. I wondered if either of them had done anything about dinner. Probably not. That was one way Simon and Leo were similar – they both seemed to think that cooking was women's work.

'Have you discovered who has been leaving you presents yet, Annie?' Big Eye asked.

'No,' I said. 'I haven't. 'But if there isn't one tomorrow morning, then I'll know it was Pete. I don't think it was Pete though. Actually, I'm thinking of staying awake all night tonight. I thought I might be able to surprise the person who's leaving the presents.'

'And if you do surprise them, what will you ask them?' Big Eye asked.

'Why they're doing it, I suppose,' I said. 'I mean, is it just a game? Or are they leaving presents because they care for me?'

'Have you thought of asking who's leaving you the presents?' Big Eye asked.

I shook my head. 'I feel shy about asking,' I said. 'I don't know why. I'd prefer to catch them doing it.'

There was another pause. I imagined myself lying in the darkness waiting for either Simon or Leo to bring me a present. I would have to drink some very strong coffee before I went to bed so that I stayed awake.

'Who do you want the person leaving you these presents to be, Annie?' asked Big Eye.

It was the question I hadn't wanted her to ask me. It was the question that was confusing me the most at the moment. 'I don't know,' I said.

There was another silence before Big Eye spoke. I chose not to break it. 'Big Eye wishes you luck, Annie,' she said finally.

I did my best to smile. 'Thank you,' I said. 'Will I have to think of another task before the final Leaving Night?'

'Big Eye has chosen a task for tomorrow evening,' Big Eye told me. 'You will all receive your instructions for it tomorrow afternoon.'

'I can't wait,' I said, not totally truthfully. I half got up from the chair. 'Right,' I said. 'I'd better go and see to tonight's dinner. Thank you for listening to me, Big Eye.'

'You are welcome to talk to Big Eye at any time, Annie,' Big Eye reminded me.

'Thank you,' I said to her, and then I left.

To my surprise, Simon was in the kitchen making a meal when I left the Diary Room. Leo was in his usual place on the sofa. He looked deep in thought, and I wondered if he was thinking about his next story.

'Dinner will be ready soon, Annie,' Simon told me with a smile.

'Great,' I said. 'It smells lovely. Do you want me to lay the table?'

'Yes, please,' Simon said.

I went over to the drawer where the knives and forks were kept and got some out. Simon looked over. 'We'll only need two of those,' he said.

I didn't understand what he meant. 'What?' I asked.

'We'll only need two knives and two forks,' Simon told me. 'I've just cooked enough food for you and me.'

'Oh,' I said, surprised.

Across the room, Leo was looking a lot more than surprised. 'Haven't you made enough food for me?' he asked.

'No,' said Simon unpleasantly, 'I haven't. I promised Annie we would do something special together when you won that stupid poetry competition. This is our "something special". You can make your own food.'

'Why didn't you tell me earlier?' Leo said crossly.

'You didn't ask,' Simon said. 'This isn't a restaurant, you know!'

Another argument! Maybe it wouldn't be such a bad thing when all of this was over after all.

'I'm sure there'll be enough for all of us,' I said. 'I don't need a big meal.'

But Simon wasn't going to change his mind. As I watched, he carried a saucepan over to the table and began to put the food onto two plates. 'Come on, Annie,' he said. 'Bring the knives and forks. We don't want it to get cold.'

So, for the second time in two days, I sat down to eat a meal that had been specially prepared for me by a man. I now knew that Pete had wanted to show me his feelings with his food. Was it the same with Simon?

And what was going to happen *after* the meal?

But nothing happened after the meal. It couldn't because Leo didn't leave Simon and me alone. All the time we were eating, Leo was singing loudly as he made himself a sandwich. A sandwich he brought over to the table to eat.

When Simon made coffee for us and suggested we drink it outside in the garden, Leo soon followed with his own cup of coffee and sat down near us.

'Do you mind?' Simon said to him angrily.

'Not at all!' Leo said cheerfully.

'I meant, do you mind moving away? Annie and I would like some space.'

'Actually,' I said. 'I was just going in to make some more coffee.'

Simon looked surprised. 'Have you finished that one already?' he asked.

I'd remembered my plan to stay awake that night. 'Yes,' I said. 'Do either of you want another cup?'

'No, thanks,' said Simon.

'OK then,' said Leo. 'Very kind of you to offer, Annie.'

And as I went back inside, I could hear the pair of them start to argue again. They were like children.

When I took the coffee out, Leo pulled a face when he drank his. 'This is strong!' he said. 'Do you want us both to be up all night or something?'

I didn't reply, and soon after that Leo was called to the Diary Room.

'Alone at last!' said Simon, moving his seat closer to mine and reaching out to take my coffee cup away.

This time Simon didn't give me a chance to talk about food or even to think. He began to kiss me straight away. It was a very nice kiss, a very nice kiss indeed. But although I enjoyed it, I'm afraid there was a part of me that felt terribly embarrassed about the millions of viewers watching me and Simon kissing. My mum watching me and Simon kissing! But I hoped very much that Janine and Gloria were watching. Especially Janine. She would be *so* jealous!

At last Simon broke away to look down at me. 'Sweet little Annie,' he said softly. I think he was going to kiss me again, but at that moment Leo returned.

'Oh, sorry,' he said. 'Did I interrupt something?'

Before Simon could answer, I got to my feet. For some reason, I badly needed to escape. 'Actually,' I said, 'I was just on my way to bed. See you in the morning.'

I did go to bed, although I wasn't at all tired. I suppose that was partly because of the strong coffee, but also I couldn't stop thinking about Simon kissing me. I'd liked Simon for ages. He'd always been friendly towards me, but he hadn't given any sign that he wanted to be more than a friend before. His feelings towards me seemed to have changed. It was very confusing.

After about an hour, the others came to bed. I still wanted to find out who was leaving me the presents. Tomorrow was the last day, so if I didn't find out by the morning, I might never find out. I kept myself awake by thinking about the museum. I played a game, imagining each room in the museum and all the things in it. If I made a mistake and forgot something, I had to start again. There are a lot of things in the museum, so this kept me busy. But as time went past, it got more and more difficult to stay awake.

I only realised I'd fallen asleep when something woke me up. Someone was getting out of bed. I kept perfectly still, waiting for whoever it was to come over to my bed to leave a present. But he didn't come over; instead he left the bedroom. When he returned two minutes later and got back into bed, I realised he must just have needed the bathroom.

The next thing I knew, all the lights were on and I was alone in the bedroom. It was morning, and by the looks of things, I had overslept. Feeling annoyed with myself, I looked down on my bed to see if there was anything there. There was something. I picked it up and looked at it. It was a key, cut out of paper. A key. What a strange present. What did it mean? And who had left it? Simon or Leo? Was I ever going to find out?

Chapter 9 *Truth dancing*

Saturday – the last day in the House – was a long day. I felt strange being around Simon after that kiss. I wasn't sure what to say to him. I didn't know what the kiss had meant, and I felt confused. But I was never alone with him anyway. Leo was always there. I don't think any of us could believe it was our last day in the House.

Finally, in the afternoon, Big Eye called Simon into the Diary Room to give him the instructions for the final task.

'Right,' he said to Leo and me when he came out. 'The final task is a dance competition between me and Leo.'

'You mean you and I have to dance together?' asked Leo.

Simon looked annoyed. 'Of course not! We both dance with Annie. She learns the tango with me, and the jive with you.'

I was immediately worried. 'Wait a minute,' I said. 'I'm not a very good dancer. I can't learn both the tango and the jive!'

Simon smiled at me. 'You'll be fine with me,' he said. 'I *am* a good dancer.' He looked back down at his piece of paper. 'Leo and I each have an hour's practice with you, and then the actual competition begins at seven o'clock.'

'But how will we learn the dances?' I asked. 'Do you know how to tango?'

'No,' Simon said. 'But Big Eye has provided us with instructions for both dances. I'm sure it won't be difficult to learn.'

'Well, I can't do the jive either,' said Leo. 'And guess what? I'm sure it will be *very* difficult to learn. I'm a useless dancer.'

'Oh dear,' said Simon with an unpleasant smile. 'I *am* sorry to hear that. Come on, Annie, we might as well start now.' Without waiting for me to say anything in reply, Simon stood up and walked towards the kitchen area. 'The floor in here will be excellent for dancing.'

I got up slowly. I didn't want to do it. I knew I was about to look stupid in front of millions of viewers. Again. I'd been telling the truth when I said I wasn't a good dancer, a fact Simon was about to find out for himself.

'Don't let him order you about too much,' Leo advised me.

I didn't like to smile at him because Simon was looking cross. 'Annie is going to have fun,' he said.

'That's order number one, Annie,' Leo told me.

'I suggest you study your instructions, Leo,' Simon said, and then he turned his back on him, bending his head over his own instructions.

While I waited, I tried to remember what I knew about the tango. I knew it was from Argentina, and a bit like a piece of theatre. I'd seen it danced on television before, but I had never, ever dreamt of trying it myself.

'Right,' said Simon to me after a few minutes. 'In the tango the man and woman have to hold their bodies very straight, and they move with quick, sudden movements.' Simon held his back very straight to show me what he meant. 'It's a dance about sex.' Behind him, Leo laughed, but Simon pretended not to hear. 'Sometimes it can even be about murder,' he continued. 'It's always a dance about fire and heat. But the most important thing of all is that neither the man nor the woman must *ever* smile. They must remain serious at all times.'

That was the hardest thing for me to do, as we were learning the dance. Oh, the dance steps were hard enough – I wasn't good at them at all. But I was really hopeless at staying serious.

'It isn't funny, Annie,' Simon told me over and over again. 'I don't know why you're laughing.'

'I'm sorry,' I said. 'It's probably because I'm nervous. I always laugh when I'm nervous.'

'Well, try a little harder, please,' he said.

So I tried, but it was no good. When Simon looked at me as if he wasn't sure if he was going to kiss me or kill me, I couldn't help laughing again.

Simon looked cross. 'Are you sure you're trying, Annie?' he asked.

'Yes,' I told him. 'I really am.'

'Well, try even harder,' he said. 'I told you: this dance is about sex and murder. It's serious.'

I did try, very hard. But I was so busy thinking about not laughing, I got the steps all wrong.

'No!' Simon said, clearly very fed up with me by then. 'Not like that, like this! I thought we'd learned that bit!'

'I'm sorry,' I apologised again. And again. By the end of an hour I badly needed to take a rest. But Simon wanted to carry on practising.

'I need to sit down, Simon. My feet hurt,' I tried to tell him, but he wouldn't listen.

'In a minute,' he kept saying. 'Let's just go over the last bit again.'

I don't know how long it went on for, but then suddenly Leo reappeared and came over. 'Your time's up, I think,' he told Simon, leading me away towards the sofas.

'There you are, Annie,' he said. 'Put your feet up.' After I had taken my shoes off my poor, hurting feet, I did just that.

I didn't say anything for a while. I was too busy thinking. The dance practice with Simon had been really unpleasant. Simon hadn't seemed to care about me being tired. He'd just gone on and on, telling me what to do and complaining when I got it wrong. I'd never thought about it before, but Simon was a bit like my boss, Mr Penforth. He expected me to work very long hours, and for no extra pay too.

'I still have to learn the jive with you,' I told Leo at last.

'It's OK,' Leo said. 'We'll just make it up.'

I suppose he was just being nice because he knew I was tired, but suddenly I felt annoyed with him. 'Don't you want to win?' I asked him.

And suddenly I realised I often felt annoyed with Leo. It was because I wanted him to … well, to *want* things more, I suppose. He didn't really seem to care about anything very much. But he must care about his writing, because he was successful at it. He couldn't be successful if he didn't care.

'I'm never going to win a dance competition against Mr Perfect over there,' Leo said.

'You might,' I told him, standing up. 'Don't be so pessimistic. Come on; you should at least try.'

'Oh, OK then,' he said.

So we began to practise, and it couldn't have been more different to dancing with Simon. With Simon it had all been very serious. I'd felt afraid of doing anything wrong.

But with Leo it was completely different. We got it wrong all the time, but we laughed about it.

'Sorry!' said Leo every time he stood on my feet.

'Not so fast!' I cried, as he danced us in a circle so quickly the room started to go round and round.

As dancers, we were hopeless, but it was great fun. I hadn't laughed so much since the spaghetti dinner.

But eventually practice time was over, and we had to get ready for the real thing. The competition started as arranged by Big Eye, at seven o'clock. Once again, we were given clothes to wear. My dress was black with a big skirt that moved around my legs as I moved. I loved it. Simon had tight black trousers and a tight black shirt and looked extremely handsome. Leo ... well, Leo had a tight *pink* shirt and tight *pink* trousers and looked ... stupid. Really stupid. Simon did all that exercise and looked after his body. But Leo was tall and thin with a bit of a stomach. The pink did not look good on him at all, and he knew it.

I tried not to laugh, but I just couldn't help it. Simon laughed too. 'You look like some kind of animal that lives under the ground,' he told Leo unkindly. 'A worm, that's what you look like. A worm!'

I watched Leo's face. For just a very short time he looked hurt. But then he laughed. 'Oh well,' he said, 'I always did like worms.'

'Me too,' I said. It wasn't the truth, but I just wanted to say something nice to Leo. I'd suddenly realised how very much I liked him. Oh, he annoyed me, and I wished he would be a bit more active, but I really liked him. And suddenly I knew I wanted *him* to win the dance competition, not Simon. Unfortunately, I knew that wasn't likely.

'The dance competition will now begin,' Big Eye told us. 'Annie will dance the tango with Simon first.'

Simon stood up and waited for me to join him. As he held me in his arms and we waited for the music to start, I looked up into his face. I don't know what I expected to see, but it wasn't what I saw. Simon's face was as empty as a piece of wood.

This time I didn't laugh once as I danced the tango with Simon. He was very pleased with me after we'd finished.

'That was great, Annie!' he told me at the end. 'I'll definitely win now!'

'Let's just enjoy ourselves,' Leo told me when it came to the jive. So that was what we did. We made mistakes and we laughed; we even put in some steps of our own that hadn't been in the instructions. It was great fun, but it wasn't the dance Leo had been told to do. I knew he would almost certainly lose the dance competition.

All three of us went to sit on the sofas to wait for Big Eye to speak to us.

'This is Big Eye,' Big Eye said. 'The result of the dance competition is to be decided by a public vote. We will tell you who the winner is at nine o'clock this evening.' There was a pause before Big Eye spoke again, and then what he had to say made us all look at each other with surprise. 'The loser of the competition will leave the Big Eye House tonight.'

Chapter 10 *Winners and losers*

None of us could believe it.

'That's not fair,' Simon said. 'Still, I shall still win. It will be obvious to the public that I'm a better dancer than you, Leo.'

Leo just looked at him.

'And then, Annie, it will just be you and me,' Simon said with a smile in my direction.

Suddenly I knew I didn't like that idea much at all. Oh, it was true that Simon was good-looking, and he could certainly kiss well. But I couldn't help thinking how horrible he'd been to Leo about his dancing clothes. And how he'd ordered me about when we'd been learning the tango. If we were left alone together in the House, I wasn't sure I would be able to think of anything to say to him.

The time until nine o'clock passed very slowly. And then finally Violet Carlton spoke to us.

'Big Eye House, this is Violet,' she said. 'The votes have been counted. The person who has lost the dance competition and who is to be the next person to leave the Big Eye House is …'

Simon was sitting up very straight on the sofa. Leo was half lying, with his hands behind his head. I was moving my foot up and down impatiently. The waiting moment seemed to go on for ages and ages.

'… Simon!' Violet finally finished.

I was looking at Simon's face as Violet spoke so I saw it turn red when he heard his own name.

'Simon,' Violet continued, 'you have five minutes to pack your bag and say your goodbyes.'

I stood up and moved towards him. 'Oh, Simon,' I said. 'I'm so sorry.'

'Yeah,' said Leo. 'You were definitely the best dancer. I'm sorry.'

Simon looked at him. 'You aren't sorry at all,' he said coldly. 'We've hated each other from the start. I don't see any need to pretend to like me just because I'm going.'

Leo nodded. 'Fair point,' he said.

Simon got to his feet. 'If you want to know the truth, I can't wait to get out of here,' he said. 'And do you know what? I don't care if I never see either of you again.' And off he went, heading towards the bedroom.

I stared after him. I couldn't believe what I'd just heard. If Simon felt like that, then what had that kiss been about? I began to walk after him.

'Leave him, Annie,' Leo advised me. 'He's obviously a bad loser.'

'No,' I said, walking on. 'I want an explanation.'

In the bedroom Simon was throwing his clothes into his suitcase. He didn't look up when I went into the room.

'You were pretending, weren't you?' I said. 'Pretending to like me.'

'Not really,' Simon said, sounding bored. 'I didn't *dislike* you. To be honest, I didn't think much about you at all until all the other girls had gone. After that, well, £80,000 seemed a lot better than £70,000, I suppose.'

'So you tried to use me!' I said angrily. 'Thanks very much!'

Simon closed his suitcase and picked it up from the bed. Finally he looked at me. 'A word of advice, Annie,' he said. 'Don't ask questions if you don't want to hear the answer.' And then he walked out.

Two minutes later, he was gone from the House – and my life – for good. Which left Leo and me on our own.

'Are you OK?' Leo was sitting on one sofa, and I was on the other. We could still hear the crowd outside. They'd gone really wild when Simon had left the House.

Leo and I were sitting quite a long way away from each other, but we were close enough for me to realise he was worried about me.

'Yes,' I said. 'I'm OK.' And I was OK. Maybe Simon had tried to use me, but it didn't matter. I wasn't really hurt, because I now knew I hadn't had any deep feelings for him.

Once I'd begun to compare Simon to Mr Penforth, my boss, I couldn't stop. Simon always thought he was right about everything, just as Mr Penforth did. Simon was nice to me when it suited him. That was just like Mr Penforth too, when he wanted me to work at the weekend, for example.

I had *really* liked Simon, but now I knew that I hadn't seen the real Simon at all. I'd just seen his good looks; that was all. But I was beginning to understand that good looks weren't that important. It was what sort of person you were that mattered.

'What you said about Simon at our spaghetti dinner,' I said to Leo now. 'You were right.'

Leo smiled. 'Ah,' he said. 'The spaghetti dinner. That was a good night.'

I remembered the spaghetti in Leo's hair and smiled. 'Yes,' I agreed. 'It was.' I looked at him. 'How did you see what Simon was really like?'

'There are lots of people similar to Simon in the writing world,' he told me. 'People who like you while you're at the top and successful. But if your next book is a failure, they don't want to know you any more.'

'False friends,' I said, and he nodded.

'Yes,' he agreed. 'But if I'm honest, I was jealous of Simon too. He's attractive and confident, and women always prefer a man like that.' He laughed at himself. 'I'm as useless with women as I am at dancing. That's why I'm a writer. Writing's easy. You can make the detective catch a murderer or the guy get the girl. Reality is much harder.'

I looked at him, realising something. 'You make a joke out of everything,' I told him. 'Why do you do that?'

'To avoid getting hurt, I suppose,' Leo answered.

'Does it work?' I asked.

'I suppose so, yes,' Leo said. 'Because it stops people getting close to me. But just lately I've been learning that it's not always a good thing to avoid being close to people.'

It was the most serious conversation I'd ever had with Leo. I wanted to ask what he meant, but Big Eye interrupted our conversation. 'This is Big Eye. The public vote to decide the winner of the Big Eye competition is now taking place. The result will be given in fifteen minutes.'

Leo and I looked at each other. Fifteen minutes. *Fifteen minutes.* If I won the competition or not, I would soon have to return to my normal life. And I might never see Leo again. Suddenly I felt really sad.

'Well,' said Leo, 'it's almost the end.'

'Yes,' I said. 'I … I'm sorry it's ending.'

I wanted one more night of talking to Leo – one last opportunity to find out about the real man behind the jokes.

I wanted to wake up the next morning to see if somebody had left me a present. Because if I woke up and found a present, then it would definitely be from Leo. And I knew suddenly that I really, really wanted it to be Leo who had been leaving me the presents. I liked Leo very much. We'd always got on well, but I'd confused those feelings for simple friendship. Leo and I *were* friends, but for me it was more than that.

'I'm sorry it's ending too,' Leo told me quietly, and suddenly I couldn't think of anything to say to him. Now I had finally realised how I felt about him, I felt shy.

There are only a few minutes left, I told myself. Say something now before it's too late.

But it was already too late.

'Big Eye House, this is Violet,' Violet Carlton said.

This was it. The result.

Leo and I looked at each other. I wanted to go and sit next to him – to hold his hand or something – but I felt too shy to do it.

'The votes have been counted, and I can now tell you that the winner of the Big Eye competition is …' As usual, Violet paused. This time the silence seemed to last ages. Then, finally, Violet spoke again: '… Leo!'

I jumped to my feet. 'Oh, Leo!' I said. 'Congratulations!' I was so happy for him. I ran over to him, wanting to kiss him or take him into my arms, but Leo just sat there. He didn't look as if he could believe it.

'Annie,' Violet continued, 'you have lost the Big Eye competition and must now leave the Big Eye House. You have five minutes to pack your bag and say your goodbyes. I'm coming to get you.'

'I … I'd better go and pack,' I said to Leo. When Leo didn't answer, I went to the bedroom as if I were in a dream. Leo had won, not me, but I didn't care. I hadn't won the £70,000, but I didn't care about that either. I'd never expected to win. But now I would have to walk up those steps from the House and face that crowd. Violet would interview me on television. But, worst of all, I still hadn't told Leo how I felt about him. Perhaps I should do it now, before I left.

But when I went back into the living area, Leo was sitting exactly where I'd left him. He didn't look like a man who had won a big prize.

'I can't believe it,' he told me. 'It must be a mistake.'

'It's no mistake,' I said. 'You heard what Violet said. You've won.'

'But why?' he said. 'Why would they vote for me?'

I knew this might be the only chance I'd ever get to say how I felt. 'Because you're funny,' I said. 'And kind.'

'No, I'm not,' said Leo.

I smiled at him. 'Well,' I said, 'you can be. You were very kind to me on our spaghetti date. If you want to, you can make people very happy.' You make me happy, I was going to add, but once again it was too late.

'Big Eye House,' said Violet, 'this is Violet. Annie, you must now leave the Big Eye House.'

The doors began to open. Leo got to his feet. 'I don't understand why you didn't win,' he told me.

'No,' I told him. 'The public chose well.'

'Annie, please leave the Big Eye House,' said Violet.

I picked up my bag. 'Goodbye, Leo,' I said.

'Yes,' he said. 'See you on the outside.'

I nodded, and then I walked through the doors. They closed quickly behind me. I walked nervously up the steps. When I reached the top, the outside doors opened, and as I walked through them, a wall of sound met me.

'Annie! Annie!' the crowd shouted. 'Annie! We love you!'

Nothing like it had ever happened to me before in my whole life, and I knew that nothing like it would ever happen to me again. I felt … like a film star.

Then Violet was there, and she was reaching out to give me a kiss.

'Annie!' she said. 'Smile for the cameras!' And I did smile, and the night sky was lit up as hundreds of photographers took pictures of me.

We walked, Violet and I, through the crowd of screaming people, and I didn't know if I wanted to laugh or cry. If they were like this for me, the person who had lost the competition, what would they be like for Leo, the person who had won the competition?

Leo. What was he feeling right at this moment?

I was soon to find out. Violet and I sat on chairs in front of the TV cameras. And there, on a very big television, was Leo, still dressed in pink, sitting in the House on his own. His face was in his hands. He looked … alone.

'Poor Leo,' Violet said. 'Look at him! You've been gone for five minutes and he's already missing you like crazy!'

'He can't believe he's won,' I said, but Violet shook her head.

'No, that's not what's wrong with him, Annie,' Violet said. 'He's missing you. I know it, the whole country knows it, and after you've seen this, you'll know it too.'

Violet pointed to the television. The picture changed from Leo, sitting alone in the living area of the House. There were lots of pictures of Leo run together to tell the story of his time in the House. But every single piece of film was about me too.

There were Leo and me playing with our spaghetti and laughing. Leo asking me his questions from his questionnaire. Leo and me laughing as we danced the jive really badly. Lots of things I knew about already. But there were other things too, things that I didn't know about. Leo looking cross when Simon was telling me what to do. Leo watching jealously from the living area as Simon kissed me. Leo in the Diary Room.

'I can't stop thinking about her,' he told Big Eye. 'She's funny, intelligent ... beautiful too, only she has no idea about that. She's always saying how hopeless she is. We're actually quite similar in lots of ways, but I don't think she's realised it yet.'

'Will you tell Annie how you feel, Leo?' Big Eye asked.

'What's the point? She won't look at me while Mr Perfect is still in the House.' Leo smiled. 'I've never been in love before. It really hurts, doesn't it? Still it will be a very useful experience for my writing.'

And lastly there was the film shot at night with the special cameras. Leo putting a paper boat on my bed. The carrot flower. The soap. The fruit face. The paper key. And every time he stood and looked down at me with … well, with love.

The film ended. Violet looked at me, and I realised my face was wet with tears.

'That is so sweet,' Violet said. 'The man has been crazy about you since Day One. How did it make you feel, watching that, Annie?'

'Sad,' I said. 'Happy. I … I don't know. I just wish he'd said something instead of wasting all this time. I had no idea he felt that way about me.'

'What would you say to him now, if you could speak to him?' Violet asked.

I didn't need to think about it. 'I'd tell him I love him,' I said.

It was the answer the crowd had wanted to hear. They let out a big scream of pleasure as I spoke. Violet was smiling all over her face. 'Well,' she said, 'I think it's time you said just that. I shall speak to the Big Eye House.

'Big Eye House,' she said, 'this is Violet.'

On the television, Leo looked up.

'Leo,' Violet said, 'Annie wants to say something to you.' And she looked at me and nodded.

I looked at Leo on the television. He was looking right back at me, and it felt as if he could see me. At the last moment, I changed my mind about what I was going to say. 'Leo,' I said, 'why did you make me that key? What was it supposed to mean?'

Leo smiled for the first time since he'd been told he'd won the competition. 'Well,' he said, 'that depends on what you want it to mean. It could just be a key to an exciting new career, or … it could be something totally different.'

It didn't seem as if millions of people were listening to our conversation. It felt as if it was just Leo and me. 'Like what?' I asked.

Leo looked nervous. 'Like … the key to my heart,' he said softly. 'To my heart and my love.'

He'd said it without making a joke and without laughing. And I knew then that he'd decided to take a chance. To give somebody – me – the chance to get close to him.

'It depends which you prefer,' he said. 'The choice is yours.'

If he'd been able to see me, he would have known that I was crying with happiness. It was such a powerful feeling, I felt as if I might explode with it. 'Then,' I said through my tears, 'I choose heart, please. Heart and love. Definitely.' And then I was laughing and crying at the same time, sitting there watching the biggest of smiles on Leo's face, and everybody in the studio was crying too. Even Violet.

'Big Eye House,' she said in a shaky voice, 'this is Violet. Leo, you have won the Big Eye competition. Get ready. We're coming to get you!'

And she took my hand and we ran back out through the screaming crowds.

'Annie and Leo!' they shouted so loudly it made my ears hurt. 'Annie and Leo!'

And then the Big Eye House doors were opening, and there he was, the competition winner, holding out his arms to me. And as I ran into them, I knew I was just as much a winner as he was.